MIKE HARDING was born into
in 1944. The tragic death of hi.
working-class upbringing have pi
for his music and 'real-life' storytelling
career, odd-jobbing as a dustman, bus condu.   ...er-itter,
Harding attended university to study Education and worked part-
time performing in folk clubs. Finally, the lure of the bright lights
proved too much and he became a full-time entertainer instead
of a teacher. Since this time, Mike has become a respected folk
musician, actor and presenter. Following on from his music, theatre
and radio success, Mike has moved into poetry, travel writing and
photography. He currently hosts a show on BBC Radio 2 and has
had over 25 books published.

Strange Lights
Over Bexleyheath

A Book of Poems

MIKE HARDING

Luath Press Limited
EDINBURGH
www.luath.co.uk

First published 2010
Reprinted 2011

ISBN: 978-1-906817-14-5

The publisher acknowledges subsidy from

 Scottish
Arts Council

towards the publication of this volume.

The paper used in this book is recyclable. It is made from
low chlorine pulps produced in a low energy, low emissions
manner from renewable forests.

Printed and bound by
Bell & Bain Ltd., Glasgow

Typeset in 10.5 point Sabon

If you don't know the trees you may be lost in the forest, but if you don't know the stories you may be lost in life.

SIBERIAN ELDER

Contents

All Talk

'All talk – just blether.' But by what else other than this chatter
Was Babel built? The Bible Belt, where corn is high
As an elephant's eye, holds fast still to a garden and a rattler,
Would crucify you for seeing us in ammonites.

Nigger, Lesbo, Commie, Paki,
Taig, Muff-muncher, Argie, Prod,
Elephant Jockey, Chink, Fudge-packer,
Towel-head, Poofdah, Jewboy, Wog.

Gaelge in the shite-smeared walls of the Kesh,
And mullahs declare a fatwah on whole lexicons.

Just air and teeth and lips? Just vowels and consonants?
Voiced palatal glide? Plosive stop? Labio-dental fricative?
The ordnance of the larynx, the smart bomb of sibilance,
Bunker buster of breath, daisy cutter of the thesaurus.

What trips off the tongue is cluster bombs, napalm, mines,
Grenades, anthrax, uranium-tipped missiles.
All talk? Another myth and old wives' tale exploded.
Take care, trust me my friend, this mouth is loaded.

Driving to the Gig
Somewhere in England, 1972

Heading due south, the winter now full in,
And evening slowly buttering the land,
The street lights flutter, sputter on.
A small town slides by, then suburbs with, on either hand,

Lit shops; a post office, then petrol pumps,
The brightly burning window of a butcher's shop;
A newsagents, a hardware store fronted
With ladders, besom brooms and mops.

Soon the houses straggle and give way to open land,
Lone houses, hamlets, farms, clusters, hives
Of the most unique, extraordinary lives.
The light from windows spools onto dark lawns;

People home from work, hang coats, put kettles on
And kiss their kids; these are the everyday,
Small, special, precious gems; the gentle pulses of our world,
That seem as though they'll beat for ever.

Another village appears, burning out of the dark;
Three teenage girls giggle their way back home,
A lone and cocksure paper boy straddles his bike,
A woman, a saucepan in her hand, turns from the stove,

A child, dressed as a princess, looks out at the night,
An old man stiffly pulls his curtains tight,
Sealing out the world, sealing in the light.
Here, and everywhere, an infinity of local epics
Go scattering; small sagas weave and web across our world.

So I drive on, a ghost, a revenant,
Through all those tales, those books, trawling
Through the shoals, slipping through the dusk,
Threading dark country miles and quiet streets
With all their infinite, endless stories.

Until I feel tonight, that here and now,
There well could be no end;
That the car and my own story will go on
For ever, through all the villages and towns,

The hamlets and the straggling farmlands
And dreaming suburbs of the night-coming world;
Through a universe of histories,
Riding on for ever through their lives,
Spinning out my own small, curious, fable.

Storm Warning

The babble began at dusk,
A BBC voice warning from the edge
Of storms out in the Irish Sea that soon would push
On, heading north by west-north-west.

By night they would be in the Dales, windows
Jabbering, trees in rictus.
       But the howling
Would be no match for the mad scirocco
In my soul. Where had this storm birthed?

Out in the still Sargasso?
In the Matto Grosso? In some quiet
Glade, had a butterfly's wing
Sliced a sunbeam and set off

A skirmish that became a battle,
Rattling the casuarinas
On St Kitts, and battering on, a high wind,
From Jamaica; the world's bat flapping, eastward?

And I sit here sensing the storm coming
To some kind of climax, holding on to the room,
The house humming, trying to decode, with paper and pen
The unutterably complex lexicons of the wind.

Paddy No One

Noone he writes, one night, tongue out, as No one
For a laugh in Longsight, on a split beer mat
With a betting shop pen. 'Noone –
It's No one – the name – you know.' But

No one sees Paddy Noone shadowed below
In the shuttering, taking a leak down in
The web of steel. The bucket swings and Casey from Carlow
Concretes him in. No sound, no shout, no one

So much as misses Noone. A navvy on the lump,
No records kept, no questions asked;
They think he's jacked, has slung
His hook for a better rate on the new by-pass.

The woman at the digs bins his few clothes, his rosary;
And a wife on a western island watches down the road,
And tells the children there'll be letters soon
From Manchester, from Daddy No one, Paddy Noone.

Old Woman On A Train

She gets on at a small, suburban halt, well dressed,
Smart, heading into town, perhaps for lunch with lady friends.
She settles herself down, straight opposite, removes
Her hat, her scarf, and last, her soft, kid leather gloves.

Then she puts up a hand to shade her eyes,
And on her wrist I see the thin blue line
Of neatly tattooed numbers (one a continental seven)
Fading on the skin's slack, ageing vellum.

And, from that winter's morning train,
The sun, an orange gong, flickering between
The trunks of red brick chimney stacks,
I see – beyond the factory backs

And houses, canals and shunting yards –
Other trains, other chimneys, and bright steel
Rails, skeined in a cat's cradle: Vienna, Lisle,
Warsaw, Krakow, Lyon, Amsterdam.

Once all roads led to Rome, and in the implacable almanac
Of those days, the iron spider's web led to the camps,
The murder factories, the ovens and the numbers on this arm,
Like smoke traced filigree across a winter dawn;

Numbers needled fifty years ago into the skin
Of this old woman, warding off the whip
Of the watery, winter sun as it cracks
Through the smoking, innocent, chimney stacks.

Brothers To The Ox

1

Born in the hungry years, two hours apart.
The midwife walks the dark miles from the road
To the dank farm under the limestone crags,
She lights the lamps, boils water, tears up linen sheets,
And kicks out the dogs and men.
Their birth cries echo round the icy combe
Where sheep lie huddled in the midnight frost,
Under a night of ice-bright stars;
And both of them are born brothers to the ox.

The land, from the cradle, has them shackled,
Bound to cart, harrow, plough, shears, tackle,
Stockholm tar, rake, bostin, scythe and sickle;
Clippings, dippings, washfold and hay barn,
Whetstone, footcock, jockey, pike and stack,
Footings, through, capstone and cripple-hole,
Yowe, tup, gimmer, wether, rush and bog.
They suck upon the nipple of a thousand years
When nothing in their vegetable world
Moved faster than a river, fetlock, bird or dog.

2

The crags' lodestone has them anchored, drags them
From running in the fields to work;
The beck they play in, dammed to dip the flock.
Their horizon: school, the fell's rim,
Chapel, and the caul of sky and stars.
Their ABC: the names of tools, beasts, fields,
Sykes, folds, ghylls, becks. Their abacus:
The dale's sheep-counting rhyme
They learn before they walk –
Yan, tan, tether, mether, pip,
Azer, sezer, akker, conter, dick.
They know the face of every wether,
Gimmer, hog and tup in their father's flock;
Bellwethers ring and call them to the fell.
Clegs, warble flies and maggots – their demons.
And they are bound to bog and crag,

All things beyond are storybook.
They cannot even tell their own small tale;
Their tongues are clagged with words the Norse
Men carried with their axes up the dale.

3

Shadows are the only clocks they need,
They read the sky, sniff storms,
Sense coming rain by the hairs upon their necks,
Hours before the warning spatters hit the fell;
Know snow by the pearl shift in the sky
And the way that noises carry across the dale;
They hear the black
Hail crackling in the clouds
Hours before ice splinters strike the crag.
Their almanac turns by the moon,
And lambing, tupping, new grass, haytime.
Their tides the rolling waves of ling
And heather and their pools, the cropped
Bright jewels of the close walled, intack fields.

4

Shit is their gold, hoarded all year,
Then buttered on the fields to coax the hay;
Hay gathered in an urgent madness,
When Mayo men come on the boat
And train to stand in line for hire
To shave the fields and sleep out in the barns.
One moonlit night they mow,
And a lost Lancaster from the other world
Toils overhead, wailing its way
Into the combe, casting casings,
Perspex, cartridges and steel
About the fell. In the fuselage
Still warm, the seven Canadian dead
Are brought down by the old horse on the sled.

5

And the years burn faster than comets,
Sure as the stars that dandle over the dale.
And they are beyond wars, beyond that other world.
Here there is only here: time defined in peat bog,
Gimmer sales, the wind and silage;
An equation to confound Einstein.

6

They tally their dead, stand silently at funerals
Like bookends, following from chapel to the grave;
The attendants of the years, now only they are left.
Winters find them wifeless working by lamplight,
Money in the mattress; hammering in fenceposts,
Walling gaps, declaring what is theirs
And no man else's. They sleep in cat naps,
Lambing, hoarding, begrudging, skimping,
Calving, milking; seeing the agent
And the ministry man and no one else.
At the Mart they stand, mute twins,
Collect their money without a word.
The ministry man explains: *the register,*
BSE, *tagging, record books* – they sell the herd.

7

One gets 'the sugar'; loses both his legs
But hobbles round on a pair the doctors give him –
A stumpy scarecrow in an old tweed coat.
His brother, shackled inch by inch by strokes,
Is turned, all down one side to stone,
Yet lugs his frozen half about their land;
A man sack, nothing but an awry bag of tricks.
One storm-black night, he tumbles in the slurry pit.
Outside, the wind rattles the black bones of
The winter thorns, and tears his garbled calls
For help to strips of nonsense, leaves
Him drowning by the lamplight in his gold.

The other stumbles on, tin-legged,
Rotting from the knees up like
A sunk post in a boggy land. Then he too dies
Ranting in his stinking bed. His last
Cries echo round the combe;
And the flock, up on the frost-bound scar,
Hear this brother to the ox,
Look up a second then graze on
Under a night of burning stars.

Edwardian Beach – Crowd Shot

They stare out from the fly-specked, fading print:
The numberless and nameless dead. Tinted
Sepia people stare into a crystal lens, a ball
That scries no future, but freezes all

Their moments, those summer's day souls
Now dust, their echoes fixed in silver salts.
Ten zones – lamp-black, through grey to arctic white –
Is enough, it seems, to fix both dawn and night;

Our small time here, this mystery beyond our reach,
That has this big-eyed child, in sailor-suit and straw
Hat, galloping for ever before the eternal tide.

So, all our summers long on this endless-seeming beach,
Smiling, we race relentlessly towards
The all-forgiving, all-obliterating light.

Children Of The Stars

They wait, the desert cold cockling their bones,
All around, the sands – an ocean whose shores are
The thin hair-line where sky meets earth –
Roll in a frozen swell across the night.

Each one's named star, as it slides slow
Over the lip of the world, marks out their dole.
When their star glims, their turn has come
To lift the cold, clear water from the well where Life
Flows in a filigree of veins beneath the desert floor,
Seeping, tortuous, drop after drop.
Assembled around the well they wait,
Willing the earth to turn, their own true star to rise,
The Children Of The Stars, humility in their every breath.

We wait, edged on the deserts of our own devising,
Not one star to our name. Unhusbanded
The dead land turns, a grey dawn falls.
In djebels of cold concrete, deserts of glass and steel
The tribes walk now, bewildered, lost;
Willing the earth to stop its turning, for
The ice to freeze again, dead birds to rise,
The poison wells to sweeten, for the woods to grow,
The bees to come again and make this world
To bloom once more somehow, miraculously
Rising, Lazarus-like, out of its concrete tomb.

A Muggletonian Prays To His God

Lord let me meet her there, full six miles high,
Beyond the manufactory sky, with its veil
Of smoke and clouds, where us, all a welter in the dale
Below, labour righteous in the tangled alleys of Thy

Will. Allow I beg, my lass to stay a lass, and not be turned,
Once in Thy bosom, into a bristle-chinned
Chap. I know Lord I have grievously sinned,
But, happily, my poor soul, weak as it is, yet burns

To see Thee face to face in Thy bright heaven. It's just –
Dus't see – I love my lass right as she is, and dunnat want
(Once our earthly husks are gone to dust)
To meet her there in Thy great heavenly room, and

Find her Charlie, not Charlotte;
Adam's rib now standing freshly made, Adam,
Knowing all the secrets of our bed.
Yet I must not seek, I know, to understand my lot,
But take what I am given, and hope to find safe haven
In Thy paradisal room six miles above the earth. Amen.

*According to the author and publisher E. L. Carr, the Victorian Muggle-
tonian Christian sect believed that Heaven was a room six miles above
the earth and that, once there, women became men. This seems just
about as reasonable as most religions I've come across.*

Becky's Welcome To The Land Of Oz

And when we finally arrived we saw a country halt;
Comforting, such a station as you only see in dreams
With flowers and shrubs in beds and tubs and, placed
About, quite welcoming, bright painted
Empty benches. On that summer day it seemed

We had come into a magic land, an enchanted park.
Blooms – topaz and ruby; trees – bronze, gold and peridot.
Somewhere a small dog barked; Toto perhaps? There was
A waiting room, cast iron lamps and, on the wall,
Timetables for the trains that never were, or would be.

There was a newly painted picket fence,
A ticket office where nobody came and went.
The station clock, whose reassuring hands
We soon saw never moved, and never would,
Smiled down on each new transport as it shuddered to a halt.

And, to complete this Technicolor wonderland
There was a zoo! A rainbow scatter of parrots,
Red squirrels, four young foxes too. And, as
The wagon doors slammed open, great, glorious light
Poured in from the far country of a fabled land.

And yet we knew, when the Ukrainians came
With their forage caps, their bull whips
And their black-glass shiny leather boots, that they
Were not Munchkins; that there were no ruby shoes;
And that this, though pretty, and most definitely not
In black and white, was probably not Kansas.

*The camp commandant at Treblinka created a small zoo near the
station, so that those about to die, as they disembarked from the trans-
ports, would not be panicked.*

The Titanic Deli

For Howard Jacobson

Ali Baba jars, glass, big as me, brimful
Of monstrous, unreal, pickled things; a wooden tub
Of roll-mop herrings, kosher wine, a slab
Of salt beef; all the smells and colours of the shtetel.

My Grandma led me through that catacomb,
That maze of matzos, bagels and letkis. In years to come
I read the narrative of the toad-skin gherkins,
The legend of the coral lox, the little man lurking

Behind the counter with his indifferent smile,
That said *My shop – Titanic Deli.*
                    Leaving Manchester
For a new life, Hyman met an iceberg and survived.
So he smiled and shrugged and decided the Creator,

Keeping him from the glacial pogrom of the waters,
Drowning orchestras and men in their daughters'
Dresses – sudden transvestites fighting for a life belt,
Killing for a lump of cork – had meant

Him to tend roll-mops, salt-beef, lox and knish
Back by Strangeways Gaol. And so he painted
His argosy's name up high, for all to understand
There was a hand that steered him here to make land-

Fall in this kosher haven in the smoky streets.
On foggy winter days his burning windows streaked
Bright, sea-washed colours on the icy fret, proclaimed his mazel
To the icebergs of buses and lorries looming through the drizzle.

Telling The Bees

The hive was a babble already, rumour flew
Fizzing through the wax-walled canyons
Of their megapolis. I heard it too:
The busy gossiping of the workers and the drones.

But I had a message to bring, the old ones said.
The green-gold way led me by water butts,
The broken cold-frames and the old plant pots,
The stand pipe and the long dry watering can,

To the glade of hives, a sacred grove
Where something god-like lived.
And so I stood, as closely as I dared,
In terror of those golden motes of fire

To whisper, 'Old Bob's gone. He died last night.'
I swear the hubbub stopped, the only noise:
My feet on cinders, scuttering back the way I'd come,
Panicked, my heart a manic, gibbering drum.

I shut the allotment gate and began to breathe
Again, the afternoon as silent as the hives,
Not daring to look back at those land-mines,
Those cluster-bombs of honeyed grief.

Rommel's Bath

The Villa Sebastian, Hamamet, Tunisia

In this '30s villa high above the reach
Of tides, where Hannibal once walked
And Roman triremes beached,
Rommel plonked his backside in hot water,
Sluiced off the dust in the cruciate marble bath,
Slotted in and plotted the slaughter,
Choreographing, on a slightly damp field map,
Between the loofah and his glass of rum,
The dance of murder in the desert sun.

Churchill followed soon after,
Slid under the suds with his cigar,
His black dog and his glass of fine, French brandy;
And his secrets: Anzac blood in the surf of Suvla Bay,
Bullets in the bricks of Tonypandy;
Dresden's elaborate ceramic sky splintered,
The city's people terror-bombed away
Melting like snowflakes in a winter garden fire.

Now on this shining day, a middle-aged couple from Brum
Look at the gilded taps and mooch and marvel,
Not knowing that two great, historical bums
Once graced the elegant, imported Italian marble.

A Bowling Green Adventure

The wood, slow bowled, meanders to the jack;
Its jealous orbit tugs it in a long swing back
To kiss the mark and settle. Satisfied, old Arnold stands
In the last of the long day's sun, gauging the run, his hand

Putting a smudge of spin upon a small life lived
Just so: no lord, no squire, no prince,
No king; just Everyman in an old,
Flat cap. And, on his last day in this world,

He wipes his forehead, looks across the park,
And stoops to bowl. His last heartbeat,
Swinging his arm in a long purposeful arc,
Lets fly the wood; awry it wobbles, biased off the green.

And the other bowlers stare as Arnold kneels
As though in prayer. Then, with a puzzled smile, he dies,
Quite gently, rolling from that northern bowling green
And out beyond the infinite summer sky.

All Pig Iron

In memoriam Lonnie Donnegan

How many boys in cold front-rooms,
Their fingers, crippled spiders, stumbling on
Steel strings, brass fretwire, fumbled for three chords:
E, A, B7, scribbling down the words
On Basildon Bond –
      I got sheep, I got cows,
I got horses, I got pigs?
'Cos the Rock Island Line is a mighty fine line,
The Rock Island Line is the road to ride...

Cold, front-room dreams,
As before the living-room fire,
Dozing fathers snored to Billy Cotton,
Red sails met the sunset,
And, in steam-filled kitchens, mothers beat
The gravy free of lumps.

Three-chord-trick fantasies. You gave the children of
The suburbs and the post-war slums
Swagger; brought to Burnley's cobbled streets
And Surbiton's mock Tudor towers these things:
The mud stink of the Louisiana levee,
Jack o' Diamonds in the stern wheeler's saloon;
Sylvie bringing a little water to the baking cotton field;
The old engineer, his hand still on the airbrake,
Scalded to death by the steam.

Brylcreemed, crepe-soled, drainpipe daydreams.
In bare-bulb, damp, church-halls across this wintry land,
Washboards and tea-chests thumped their way
To the Cumberland Gap, and a generation of Lost Johns
Started putting on the style. We built the Coolee Dam,
Fought The Battle of New Orleans,
And ran with young Tom Dooley from the law;
But mostly, we rode the old Rock Island Line.

I fooled you, I fooled you
I got all pig iron, I got all pig iron.
'Cos the Rock Island Line is a mighty fine line,
The Rock Island Line is the road to ride.

Nobody's children in cold front-rooms,
You gave us songs to sing,
You gave us dreams to dream.

Strange Lights Over Bexleyheath

Do you remember how we thought the world would end
With spindly, giant, robot legs above Big Ben?
With Martian crane flies, tower-block high, stalking
Above a boiling Thames; Putney and Dorking

Vaporised, Sidcup in flames; Romney and Hythe
Choked with the dead? How we would watch them stride,
Across the world, triumphant, turning scattering crowds to slag?
Or perhaps it was a clutch of long-forgotten eggs,

Back in the shadows of a cave, found by a shepherd
Boy. They hatch; next comes a gaggle of Grendels, hydra-headed
Monsters looming over panicked towns, doomed
Villages. TVs across the globe, above bars, in family rooms

Smelling of dinner and children, would all show
(In this Technicolour ending, folk-devil, overblown
By Hollywood for the silver screen) the dismantling
Of Man's dominion, his only earth unravelling.

New York: anarchy, looting, burning banks;
Prague: a charnel house; Moscow: all ablaze;
In Adelaide, Hong Kong, bulldozers fill mass graves.
Then all across the world, the screens go blank.

And yet it was far simpler than all that:
No alien, star-come cylinder shimmering in a London park;
Just exponential growth, a well-filled tank,
The lunatic sprawl of concrete and tarmac;

No shining metal feelers slithering out of the pit;
Just the warming ice shelf's interminable drip.
No comet bearing bacilli, no solar flash;
Just an infinity of fingers, feeling for that small key in the dash.

Visitors To The Scar Museum

They stand, befuddled by the warmth, hardly aware,
Of the uniformed attendants catnapping in hard chairs.
Outside, buses change gear, the afternoon dies, damp and cold;
The visitors wipe their feet, shake off the fog, make for the Old

Masters, where the real gems can be seen:
The classical and the mythical, the tortured and tormented;
Ophelia, Tess – the abused and the demented,
Tristan and Iseult, Catherine with her wheel.

Next door the abstract modernists may be found:
Desertion, Cuckoldry, Rape, and some minor artists –
Naive painters almost: Swindle, Trickery, Insult. The rarest
Are roped off. The visitors stand around

Remembering, comparing scars. 'You know, I've one
Could be the twin of that up on the wall; but mine
Is fading now – it's hardly there – it's nearly gone'
But after every visit, when they pull the blinds,

And the attendants swamp the rooms with dark,
The visitors move homewards through the park,
Back to their bedsits in Edwardian suburbs
Or houses out beyond the buses' terminus.

There, in the quiet hours, it comes, the panic time:
A twist or turn of phrase, a photograph, a sign,
An ornament, place name, a twist of song –
And then the scars begin to tingle, itch and throb.

In The Necropolis

Stelea and shattered columns, urns and cherubim,
Angels, broken-winged with moss-crowned heads;
Weepers and laurel wreaths, pyramids and mausoleums,
Enough stone for a city, and here the city is –
Row on row, and street on street, a city of the dead.

Yet only the moneyed dead, because the poor
(Who don't so much as scratch the looking glass
Of History) unnumbered and unnamed lie somewhere else;
This is the necropolis of an altogether other caste:

The ship men, shop men, steel men, coal men,
Lawyers, judges, merchants and their wives,
Their sons and daughters and their priests,
The generals, admirals, sea captains and the deans;
The city's great and good, all ranked and tiered they lie
Unhumbled in these mossy, tumbled streets.

Here they are found still serried in their deaths;
The mighty Empire's seed, its children and
Its servants, waiting out the years. They sleep on
In Cadaver Mansions, ears cocked for the trumpets' peal
When Heaven's portals will open and the ladders of the sun,

To the braying roar of brass will come rattling down
To Adam's earth. And they will rise again;
The shakily reassembled skulls and bones,
Lungs, lights and livers, will brush the gravemould off
To begin their elect and righteous climb to Paradise.

On this lead-grey, atheistical day it seems
Less likely, as I stand in streets of awry, fallen stone,
In avenues of bone; Skull City where the mausoleums
Are fenced off with chainlink and scaffold poles,
Barbed wire and hi-vis, Day-Glo cones.
'Unsafe – Keep Out' new epitaphs declare,
And the courts are home now to another class:
The crack-heads and the winos and the lost,
The living flotsam rolled in on the city's tide.

Here on this grey, dour, Glasgow hill –
The earth sodden, dead leaves rotting,
The city smudged below, fading and indistinct –
I note how the city's rich outreached, outbid,
Outdid each other even in their deaths,
As though their God read balance sheets
And ledgers, was impressed
By shiny boots, a well turned gamp, a tidy life
Lived on the up and justified by faith;
Mercantile and double entered,
Often on the square, as though He really cared.

Certain in life, doubtless in death
Their many mansions range about the hill.
But Time the Leveller rolls on, and everywhere
In this great hill of bones, stones tilt,
Urns lean, walls sag, stelea fall, gates rust, putti rot.

The angels suffer most, losing their wings
And praying hands to well aimed bricks.
The vandals wind and rain, and brother frost
Will bring this all in time to dust. And even so,
The finely chiselled names name none that we would know.
Who would remember them or what they did?
Who claims kin now with the 'honourables', 'esquires',
The burghers levelled by the guillotine of days
The smooth-wheeled tumbril of the years?
Their names are a lost language,
A freemasonry of gone; their epitaphs
A history of nowhere. I walk the untended way,
One man alive in a metropolis of bones.

Above the hill a chopper hovers now,
'Chuppa, chuppa' go the blades, a grey
Sound on a sunless, dying, winter day.
And two angels, seraphim in regulation blue,
Looking for the dealers and crack dens,
Patrol the air above the city of the dead.

Park Benches

We saw Venusians on park benches by the bowling green,
Marooned, beached by the tide, toothless as turtles; weak,
Sad eyes following the bowl's ineluctable roll to the jack
Backs hooped, necks wattled, legs cranky – all spectacles, flat caps
And floral frocks; while we, the immortals, hurtled round
The fountain and the bandstand, scootered fast and loud.
They, on their benches, were creatures from the Planet Old,
Where false teeth clacked and pipes were smoked,
Where stockings concertinaed, and where hands
Hurt, twiggy fingers puffy against worn, gold bands.

Now, long scooterless and greying, I sense landfall.
The cosmic tide rolls in, and though the surf is still a small
Way off, the now familiar turtles from Outerspace,
Smile and shuffle down the bench, point out my place.

Filling The Kettle

It went on first thing, a morning rite, with you the acolyte,
As the cindery ashes were blown back to life,
And we on winter dawns, dressed shivering hard,
Dancing for cold on the rag rug before the warming hearth.

From hob to pot (you would always scald it first)
Your cup of tea (two sugars), your morning thirst,
The cigarette lit from the fire – then you were slaked,
And, apron on, you set about setting about the day.

Each visitor, their foot half in the door
Would hear the kettle singing out;
Stranger, friend, priest – no matter, for
No caller ever went home dry from our house.

A cup of tea, a fresh cut slice of bread
And butter, or some cake – all this was given as read.
That was the way, back then,
When you were nearly thirty and I was almost ten.

But the cruel years ran faster than the top
I spun before the fire, hummed doggedly on
Chanting their own implacable song,
'It won't be long – it won't be long – it won't be long.'

Now you look through a stranger's eyes it seems,
And, for a moment wonder who I am; and all about
Slips into a fog of light and noise. This new-come childhood means
That we, your children, are your parents now.

I see you turn, hands lighter than a small bird's wing,
Your arm a thin branch ending in a painful clutch of twigs.
The old words now are coming back: the sink – *a slopstone*,
The settee – a *settle*. Pared to the bone

You totter on, a toddler in this jumbled, undersea world,
Enchanted by the complex mysteries of the commonplace: a girl
Passing, a bird on the windowsill. Your very breath is brittle;
No longer strength enough to even lift the kettle.

Sea Fruit

What could they know of the ocean? All
Those tribesmen hill-locked in their cwms,
Cosseted in the bare stone arms
Of the mountain; fast bound in their sunk dales

Where the limestone dripping with the candle wax
Of saxifrage, the bone-white scars and crags
Defined their world? What would a gull's song
Mean to them, or the chant of waves lapping along

The strand? He sat down by the fire, salt crusting his clothes,
And told them of mermaidens and sea snakes;
Of sailing chariots and giant whales,
Of a tarn so big its teardrop filled the world;

A tarn so big it swallowed the golden head
Of the sun each night, eating its burning tail;
So big the moon dragged herself out, drenched
And fecund with it, scattering a shower of stars.

He held the heavy shell up to their ears
'Listen,' he said. 'This is the singing of the sea.'
The tunnelled, creamy whorls of the conch
Carried the susurration of a distant surf,

Whispers of blown foam along a windy shore.
Locked in the shell's coils the sirens sang,
Murmuring in the ears of the mountain men;
Singing the kiss of combers on a pebble shore,
A curlew's caoin, the slow, eternal churning of the seas.

In the conch's song, the story of elsewhere;
In the shell's pages, the texts of imaginary oceans.

History Lesson

Oi the Long March of the Everyman

They lied, saw order (constant as eye and hook)
Ordained, sure as the monstrance;
Happenstance – a word not in their book.
Instead they saw: (take note now,
Write this down – for marks boys)
Manifest Destiny,
The White Man's Burden,
The Civilising Rod,
The Long March of Everyman,
And not forgetting, Pax Brittanica.

Boys, it was the warp and weft of Empire,
A world woven from cotton, rubber and teak,
Of oil and ivory, slaves and silks and spice,
Gold and sugar and tea, and all things nice,
Brought by kind gentlemen in ironclads
Through all the perils of the Seven Seas
To where a small, fat lady dressed in black
Sat on a gilded throne.
                    So spin the globe
And see the pink wash over half the world,
The Empress elevated, and the elephants
The doodah with the howdahs,
The palaver with the Rajahs.
Observe more recent newsreels, flickering narratives:
A queen with a bouquet and smiling picanins,
The royal yacht rides in the offing. Take the pith
Helmets, ostrich feathers, smiling governors.
And, at the jungle's edge a croquet lawn
Where parasols, cucumber sandwiches
Tiffin, amahs and coolies may be found;
Straw boaters, ties and flannels will be worn.
And all of this leads to a sunrise where their God
Holds out his bloody hands to encompass all
Their righteous, self-fulfilling world.
They failed to see the bodies strapped across

The English canon mouths, the hands cut off and dumped
In our own Empire's bucket.

For this has always been their dancing tune:
(Ready boys, cock a leg, jig it out
Before we send you to the front.)
1815 The Treaty of This,
1726 The Act of That,
1907 The Congress Of The Other,
The War Of Jenkins' Ear and Hitler's Balls.
And what then of the Great?
George Third – a human frog,
Alexander the Great – a drunken thug,
Napoleon – a short-arsed fool,
Henry Eighth – a syphilitic baboon,
Pius Twelfth – an anti semite Pilate,
Washing his jewel-encrusted fingers in the bowl;
Churchill – a manic boozer with his own black dog;
And all of them still waltzing as the clock
In the school hall ticks on towards
The midnight meeting in the Valley Of The Bones.

No march, only Ozymandias drunk
And dancing in the ruins and dust,
The Long And Shambling Stumble
Of Everyman to the Pit.

Bolstered with certainties the paedophile
Monsignor holds the monstrance and the pyx,
Sings of the blood of martyrs, but draws closed
The curtains on the Inquisition, the rack,
The burning women and the boiling pitch.

They lied but did it beautifully
In soaring plain chant and in Jesuitical prose.

Put a donkey in a dog collar – you have religion,
Stick a pig on a midden – you have government,
Chain a dog before the door – you have the law,
Stick a crown on a turd – you have (fanfare please) royalty;
Hanging out the bridal sheet above the mob,
Blinding them with finery, lineage and cant.
Behind them: brown-nosed buffoons and place men
Are climbing the shit ladder, a daisy chain
Of hands on daggers in backs. While in the city,
In their towers of brass, the alchemists turn gold
To lead, but not before they've filled
Their sow's ear pockets well and fled the scene
To hide their funds in hedges
Where the grass is always green.

Only the worms are honest,
Only the maggots are true.

May the worm that tunnels through the dung
Beneath the trotters of the pigs,
Bring down this hollow tower of shit
And teach us all, one day – humility.

To The Source

It's up there in the hills somewhere,
Lost amongst cool pines, their straggled heads
Tangled in the clouds. In some high grove
Where the rock clefts, and soft moss fringes
The labia, it comes languid, dribbling down
The stone lip, slipping into the pool.

It is the real stuff; air-clear, touchstone,
The real McCoy, the pure drop.
Untainted lexicons move with the breeze,
Whisper their truths amongst the prattling leaves.

Up there with hawk and raven its deep pools
Hold speckled trout, the salmon thrashes
Up the falls to scurry to her redd, the otter
Slughead, sinuous, lollops to the bank, dives and is gone.

By the time it hits the lowlands,
Oxbows slug-slow through sunk farms,
Past factory backs, new raw estates, dull towns,
It is clagged with the tedious meanders of its going.

At the sea's reach it danders through mud flats,
Sidles by sandbars scribed with seagulls' feet, rats'
Claws. It comes to wander by sunk hulks,
Old crates, awry cranes, crab shells, dumped cars,
Scabbed iron piles. By then it will be bellyful of history;
Foul, scummed, festering, poisonous perhaps.

Who then will know of that split rock,
Those mountain pines, that song
Still whispering, licking,
Nudging at the spring's fat, mossy lips?

I Bin Sad 4 Yers and Yers

Words found chalked on the wall of a one-time childrens'
home in Jersey

Words on a cellar wall – a mantra no one read;
Fading in a cellar's whispering damp – whimpers no one heard;
Interred in a mass-grave of forms – names no one knows;
Lost in a desert of diktats – the children abolished.
All, all abandoned, Hansel and Gretel-like,
To the gingerbread house of care
In the forest of self-righteousness.

The hand whose child chalked that,
Whose soul scrawled out that scream,
Whose body was on fire with cold and fear,

Is gone.
　　　　But those few words scald hotter now
Than all the stars that fleck the universe.
Good Christians rejoice, Christ did not mean
You when he spoke of millstones and the deep.

Rest easy in your fat, fine, feather beds
Your warm, still, safe-as houses;
While the children in the cellars scream and scrawl
Their secret stories out, write them in tears of fire
On the wet, cold, indifferent stone.

At first I think there is no hole in Hell
That's deep enough or dark enough
To hold you; until it comes to me that once, perhaps –
After some uncle buggered you,
Or some loved one beat you half to death –
You too picked up a piece of mortar chalk,
And with countless other hands across the world
Scratched out in burning stars on some dark cellar wall,
Calling to a god with long-deaf ears,
The prayer, 'I bin sad 4 yers an yers.'

The Old Ones

On the prom they read the Sundays in their cars,
The springs they ride on – a begrudging calm,
Prickling trivia, carping nowtiness.
'You always think that you know best!'
'That was the year my mother died, so I should know.'
'You'll do what you want, any road.'
'In any case, you never liked our Flo.'

Islanded they totter, tapping their way
Crabby in crimplene towards the unimaginable night.
When one goes there will come the ghosts:
A severed limb still aching; a house door
Stopped that was banging in the wind;
A tap no longer dripping in the sink,
And just one cushion waiting be primped.

Millstone Grit

Stone the bones, and stone the skin
Of these brown towns come tumbling in
All higgledy down the moorland hills.
Pooled in the valleys, villages,

Cities and towns have grown, strange fungi
In ghyll, syke, dean and dell.
A second skin of buildings – streets
Of houses snaking up the hillside; mills

And bridges, farms and barns, houses
Shops, churches, chapels, schools, town halls,
Whole cities, nowt but dark smoke-blackened stone;
Hand-cut lintels, mullions, walls,

Flags and roof slates, sinks and sills.
All these hill towns born of cut
Gritstone, butter-yellow; so much that
It is a wonder that the hills

Aren't hollow. And perhaps
Some day to come, in the summer heat,
When rosebay willowherb seed heads
Cloud the drowsy air, the whole Pennines

Kit and caboodle, in a gentle puff of dust
Will sink quite softly, with a sigh, collapse,
Implode into what in time becomes the steppes
Of Rochdale, Oldham, Huddersfield and Halifax,

Settling serenely in the summer air
Like a silk hat on a Bradford millionaire.

The Rain Would Drive You To Drink

Not just the rain: wind, mist, snow, fog,
Hail, sleet, thunder, ice, frost,
Lightning (sheet, ball and fork)
And even, so it seems, sunshine.

Once opening a bar door on a brass-bright, summer's day
Looking for Joe, I saw only the lurkers on high stools.
Like heifers in a winter stall they stared at me,
A silhouette framed in a furnace door,
Then turned back to the matter between their hands,
Snug in their smoky otherworld.
Old days the fairy music drew men under hills
Or into fairy forts, bewitched and wandering,
To send them gibbering home with tales to tell.
But now the wide screen and the Lotto seem to serve as well.

But the rain set in the rot,
The everlasting, whooring, forty shades of rain,
And the colonising boot,
That never lets up, even on this long midsummer day,
Of the grey Atlantic skies, smudged soot,
That have kicked this sodden August all to hell.
The Inuit, they say, have forty words for snow.
The Irish in their lexicon should have
A hundred words at least for rain.
        A soft day and the hagfish dark come early
Sucking all the colour from the land.
The harbour lamps come sputtering on,
I drive along to Joe's and see in the half-light,
Courting the ditch, a staggering man.
Head down and coatless in the mithering rain,
He walks like a sick calf, no thought but for home.
And there: a wife, the TV on, his dinner dry
And covered with a plate, and kids ready to fly
His raddled rage, his windmill fists.

He lurches, stumbles, teeters on the ditch's edge,
Dances, mumbles, spins, then lifts his head,
And curses spatter out; on God, the rain, the bogs,
And the dead cert that fell this afternoon at Doncaster.
The maledictions rattle his teeth,
Cannoning like comets from his open maw,
Spluttering out across a Connemara
Summer sky the colour of a dead nun.

A Calvinist in the Dales

1971 – in reply to Jack Clemo's 'A Calvinist in Love'

When I have loved you country fashion
By drystone walls where
Wind and the moors' bare
Flanks claim kin with all our passion,

We will share with older gods
The rites of earth
The solemn mirth
Of this whole flux of ling, heather, clod

And peat, bracken, wind and sun;
The splash of stars
And flasks of carved
Flowstone that cup the running

Beck. And I will ask no more this day
But that the years
Don't cloy with fears
That need more than this clay-

Bed love on heather under skies
Where plovers reel and flick
And larks burst out and up, bright,
Slow falling sparks of this first eversong.

Fox, Lark and Leaf

Marmer Sunter soldiers on,
At eighty eight a chime child of the century. Alone
But for the barn cats and his dogs
And stock. He farms High Crags, lost
For half the year in low cloud or high mist;
The rest lost in the song of curlew,
Peewit, oyster catcher and the one
He always stops to listen to:
The carolling, eye-mote, spiralling spark
And shimmer of a sky-hung meadow lark.

He times his year by lambing, gimmer
Sales, and the chuntering bark of guns in heather.
The welfare woman comes and cleans and scolds,
Wipes chicken droppings from the kitchen table,
And checks the larder out for mould.
'He shouldn't be alone you know. He's just not able.
It's such a scrow! There's a sister in Penrith,
And another out at Brough –
Not married, but wouldn't you think...'
Rough and ragged bogland, enough

To span the head stock of the dale
Before the cusp, beyond the which
You pass into another dale, another world,
Edging this in rushy acres. Still
He steers his spindly heifers across his sodden land
And in days of paraffin lamps
And oilskins lets it all pass by:
Two world wars, Suez, the bomb, Man on the moon –
All not much more to him than cattle mart tales;

And the planes that leave snail trails
Of silver in the blue-clear, dale-head sky
Are no more than the scratches
On the kitchen window pane.
Fox feral, when he tumbles like a leaf
In autumn, lies alone for days,
The police will find, when they
Kick down his door and clear away
What's left and free the blowflies,
A corduroy millionaire, owned by
The land he never rose above; they will find
The lord of three hill farms, who signed
All forms and documents with his mark:
An infant's schoolroom drawing of a meadow lark.

Cairn Makers

Stone on stone and word on word –
All you can hope for at the close of everything.
Micho Russell's, 'It's all a bottle of smoke,'
Alexander's bones and brittle legends,
Dusty histories and Caesar schoolboy jokes.

Inch on inch the tides come, inch on inch they go,
Moons span the line from headland to the hills,
Day follows day and all that you can hope
Is that, when all the mourners go their way, still

The cairn will be there. Cairns mark the way
On and off the fell; those stone fists clenched
On the crags' rim have a narrative, they say
'I too came this way, and this is what I did

In my small time here, my long time gone.'
And this is all we can any hope to do:
To leave a marker on the great fell of the world
Word on word, stone on stone.

Galway–Dublin Bus 1997

A winter's afternoon, grey gales and rain
Scudding the bus on eastwards through
Pinched places with small names,
Where buffeted people, heads down, blew

Along the empty streets of dour, damp, market towns.
The midlands rolled for ever; rain and wind
Lashed them, smeared and smudged them down
The Galway Dublin road. Then we drew in

To somewhere small and grey, with several pubs,
An Oifig Post, a news shop with its Lotto,
And a grotto with a Virgin in need of a good rub
And a lick of paint. My face rested on the window,

Half asleep. Then something caught my eye, and I looked up
And saw a hand draw back the upstairs curtain lace,
And someone in that small gap staring at the bus,
And I read the certain story of that face:

Old parents to be nursed, a lover in the States
The letters drying up as surely as her womb.
Now she haunts the church and rises late
To spend her days ghosting from room to room;

A life stitched by the town's relentless hand,
Mocked by each new dawn. And now the face is leeched
And hungry as the stars, as lonely as a bleached
Branch, driftwood on an empty strand.

The bus revved up, and we pulled out, leaving
Behind these things: a cloud of our black smoke,
An Oifig Post, a grotto, and two virgins
Staring down the darkening Dublin road.

This Road

The rain was coming sideways and the wind
Had ripped the skin from off the ribs of the day;
Light failing in a rolling sea of bog, a land
Where only boulders grow. Glencolumbkille –

Out there somewhere in the watery slather,
But where I didn't know; the map
As much use as a chocolate tea pot.
Alone in a wilderness made infinite by mist,

In a land where they plant stones and harvest rocks –
A cottage, turf smoke writhing from its stack.
An old man stooped, the stoker with a sack
Across his shoulders filling a creel with turf from off

The reek. I wound the window down, the rain sailed in,
He stood, his stance a question. 'Where will this road
Take me?' I asked him, waving vaguely at the moor
I knew was somewhere out there in the mist.
'This road will take you anywhere you want to go.'
He nodded, hutched the creel and slammed the door.

The Nowhere Train

When they scanned my curious island
I got my ticket for the nowhere train.
On Spyglass Hill magnetic fingers and wires,
Hawkins and Silver, looked for Flint's Fist in vain,

Found instead old Ben Gunn pounding an erratic drum
Falling off the perch, buying the farm of Kingdom Come,
Too much Christian bread and cheese and liquor,
The doctor smiled, I fingered my fresh-printed ticket.

They said they would ship me to the ward;
But I know the ward I've seen the charts.
It's there the Nowhere Train departs
Rattling on into the final, absurd night,

Leaving behind a station of cupboards, drips
And catheters, puckered grapes, old magazines,
And nurses stripping beds to pave the way
For other travellers like me who will see
That the tickets actually only go one way.

The Irish For Oasis

Crossing the deserts of North London
On a Sunday summertime, they go,
By griddle pavements and brick terrace ovens
To the Favourite in Holloway Road.

After-Mass caravans of baggy-suited men; rolled
In their jacket pockets, truncheoned Irish Posts.
Pints in the dark room, and Sweet Afton smoke
Whorls in the window light, spools, coils.

Martin the fiddler gives a nod, the squeezebox wheezes
Out a chord, and they jig it out: *Hitler's Downfall.*
Men move like palm trees in a cooling breeze,
This pub a haven in a yellow-brick dust bowl.

Outside, a Kalahari of burning tarmac streets;
And, in the desert beyond this small oasis,
The smell of English beef and Sunday roasts
As London jigs and twitches in the heat.

Wyrdewurke of Giants

*The buildings left behind in the English landscape by the
departing Roman Empire were called by the
uncomprehending tribes that followed after 'the
wyrdewurke of giants.'*

When the tribe come paddling through the city streets
Long, long after the giants have all gone,
What they will do is gape and gawp
And try to fashion words for all this marvellous ruin.
They will skim their skin canoes by upper floors,
The cracked and falling mirror glass
Of marble banks and offices. Slime will patina
The rusting steel, the logos, and the mantras
The tribe no longer will be able to decode:
Starbucks, BP, Sony, Toshiba, Rio Tinto Zinc;
But no Rosetta Stone will be there to link
The patois of the tribe with these strange marks.

Mud will carpet then the rooms of CEOs,
And monstrous fish, and things that have no name,
Will nuzzle and suck, searching for food,
Seeking the mutant molluscs that have made
The pediments and steel struts their home. A giant wheel
For which their water world has now no use will lie
Half-drowned; the glass snout of a priapic
Ruin will sniff at the ash-coloured sky.
Warm rain will fall upon the works
Of the giants. On their way back to high land
The tribe leave offerings on the four-faced tower,
Honey, meat, burning incense, some flowers.

The tower has bells that ring when the hot wind blows
From the North, and the black birds rise like smoke
Over the waters. Nothing was left of the giants,
Only the stones and things that have no meaning now:
Glass boxes, strange wheeled boats on the marshy land.

And nothing else? The stories all died with the ones
Who knew the meaning of the marks; there were no songs,
No stories. With all the myths and histories
And legends carried on a wire, the chain so easily broke.
After the great flood and the fall of all, there was the End
Of All; what Gods there were had failed them.
And so they vanished, those strange days,
Came to an end in easy anarchy.
The world turned feral with the great
And small eating each other so the old ones say.

These days, the tribe, armed with an apronful of words,
Fishes, fights and forages amongst the islands
Of a long-drowned world, and fashions huts
And hunts all through the wyrdewurke of the giants.

Mothers Of All Wars

Come back with your shield, or on it
Spartan mother to her son

It will be the mother of all wars
Saddam Hussein

They empty their wombs into the mouths of guns,
Wave on wave of smiling children skip
Into the playground of the mad. Why rush to pick
Him up when he tumbles, soothe his graze, mother?
Why bother? Why fuss? His days are set; meat for the metal.
Petals of flesh rain from the sky, somebody's boy
Is cooked to a turn in the tank's turret,
The roast head seeming to grin as though
Quite happy and bemused. We mistake
The rictus of our terror for a grin of joy.
Whose boy? And does it matter? Why worry?
Come on mothers – hurry!
Make more meat for the madmen, medals
With bright ribbons will be yours. Glorious
Wars: that's what wombs are for.

And the Grand Old Fools of history have
Their pictures painted: riding on
White chargers; sitting in fat arm-
Chairs with cigars; standing heroic
Against a smoke-dimmed sky – how glorious!

The artists' brushes? – the bones
Of your babies; the oils? – their rendered fat;
Pigments? – the scarlet scream of blood, the blue-
Purple of gangrene, the green of grave-
Mould, yellow of rotting flesh.
Oh there's no end of colours, mother.

Austerlitz to the Zulu Wars, Stalingrad to Agincourt,
'But, you know, that's what young men are for.'
Said the mad Little Corporal with the Chaplin tash.
Kosovo to Crecy, 9/11 to My Lai,
Baghdad to Leningrad, Dresden to Coventry –
The generals' coaches run on roads of meat.

And mother, can you find the pieces in
The dust? What meat is yours, and what is hers,
The mother of your son's young enemy?
And can you pluck them from the mud, and piece
Them back together in the jumbled jigsaw of the ossiary,
Breathing life back once again into the bloody, mouldered bones
So they may suck once more your Spartan breasts?

On The Lump

A lorry drops him off at the end of day,
Soil and sweat on Friday's suit, his boots clay-
Clagged. In his one-bar, one-bulb
Room he has a swill, then heads out for the pub,

A fourpenny bus ride down to High Stool Hall.
Mahogany, etched glass, the warmth, the craic,
The schooners that turn time around, blunt pain, so that
Mayo's whispering ghost recedes beyond the city's pall.

But the lips of the women are not for him,
The breasts of the women are not for him,
The smiles of the women are not for him,
The love of the women is not for him.

No warm back to spoon into, only
Cold, soiled sheets, in a damp, rank room
That reeks of piss and loneliness. But a lagoon
Of stout would not put out the lonely
Desert thirst of this rambling, navvy man,
Nor a universe of moons light up his dark.

And so he's out again into the night;
A whistle from a far-off train, bark
From a somewhere dog; buying painted smiles
From peroxide, shivering girls;
Love by the pound in Hanky Panky Park.
'Come on Paddy – I'll show you a good time.'

And the full moon scuds through the broken cloud
Above the Salford alley where the bargain's struck,
The same old moon that limes Croagh Patrick, and
Silvers the wind-ragged, empty streets of Kiltimagh.

Kiltimagh: pron cull-she-muck; a town in County Mayo.
Croagh Patrick: pron. croak; the holy mountain of Ireland.

Country Bells

They call out over Sunday England still,
Singing them to church across the shires,
The dales, the fenlands and hills.
On summer Sabbath mornings the bright peals
Sail on over village greens and playing fields,
The water meadows and the fells, where limestone
Scars send back their tumbling echoes.
But an ageing crew now answers to the call;
Arthritic, bent, part of a way of life that seems
Quite strange, quaint almost: King and country,
The squire in his hall, and each man in his place;
Like the war memorials to the Afghan wars
The crumbling airfield and the overgrown pillbox,
These are echoes of a different, mythic time.

The fat man, shirtless, waters his smooth lawn,
The baseball-capped boy-racer waxes his new ride;
Families get ready for the new cathedrals:
The garden centres and the shopping malls.
The young mums jog by with their iPods on,
Hardly remark the suited and the hatted as they pass,
The greying and the bald who make
Their way, quite slowly, to the cool, the dark, the brass
Those naves that hold their mailed marbled tombs,
The lectern with its eagle, and the corner with
The Lego for the mum and toddler group.
Half in, half out of time, the quiet itself
Waits for them coming with an air
That smells of history, damp stone and fresh-cut flowers.

And there they sit on waxed pitch pine and oak,
Enacting something old and needful, kneeling where
Their fathers and their mothers knelt;
A dwindling band who pass, fewer by the year,
The stone jamb where the archers left their marks
While sharpening their arrows for Flodden on the stone;
Past the ancient yew whose narrative,
Like that of the stained glass and the carved heads,
Grows fainter and more tangled year by year.

Train Times To The Hospital

I found today, tucked away in an old, leather
Wallet: a raffle ticket, an Irish fiver,
And, typed out on a worn and folded slip of paper,
The train times to the hospital;

With a good few changes possible
At Preston, Lancaster or Crewe, the faster
Being Lancaster where the Scots express
Would get me through to London on time

To cross to Waterloo,
And out on a suburban line
To the madhouse where they kept you caged,
A bright bird in the Fairy Feller's house.

To see Mad Tom of Bedlam
Ten thousand miles I travelled,
Mad Maudlin goes in dirty clothes
Her soul it is unravelled.

And I see those times and numbers now
Those digits signifying nothing
But the art of the possible,
And all I remember is the silver rails
And the inner tears I'd weep
Silent weeper, a sea for every sleeper.

The Barford Angel

All you need for heaven is a rickety bike
And the wooden wings of a dulcimer
Strapped across your back, trapezoid in the gloom.
He looked, they said, like
Some kind of peddling angel
Wheeling along the country lanes,
His wings outstretched, cycling
Through the night, working himself up
To a long take-off. And take off he surely did,
Lifting the dancers with him
Spooling them in with his notes,
Spinning them round the room,
Leading them out of the village halls
And old pub bars and up
To dos-y-dos and strip the willow around the stars.
Then it was back on his old bike,
Off home alone, his jangle-box wings
Still keeping him aloft,
Carrying the bright flame of music
On his Raleigh handlebars,
Chain whirring, strings softly jingling,
Raggle taggle through the country night.

*Billy Bennington was a hammer dulcimer player, his nickname was
The Barford Angel*

Northern City, Summer, Sunday

(Late August, 1951) in memonam George Melly who liked this poem

Thistledown the wind, there comes a flock
Of rose bay seed heads from the bomb
Sites, swirling, fuming around the furnace of
The red brick, Sabbath streets. The town hall clock

Has softened, it folds and slips to slither
Down its tower. Time bends and wobbles
In the summer, Sunday heat. Air shimmers;
Lines of backstreets meet in a glaze of cobbles

And a shimmering mirage of hills
Of trembling, blue-remembered slate.
And I, a solitary, school-free child,
Wander these vacuous city streets. In days

To come I didn't baulk at Dali's wilted
Watches, Chirico's clown towns; for I
Had seen the old Masonic Hall trembling
And a bronze Victoria and Albert bending,

Boogying in the glassy, sashaying air.
Brass band music from somewhere,
And empty streets and smokeless factory stacks,
Canyons of burnt sienna, dark umber back-to-backs;

A Lazarus chapel rising from a swamp of graves,
A cotton-mill sailing, ship shape, over waves
Of ziggurat, spinning-shed glass. This was clearly
A mutable world, a place in flux, unstable. Here

Brass bands play, their tubas all on fire; a rose
Is never a rose, no pipe a pipe. Here
Magritte at any moment might appear,
In a town clerk's bowler hat, smoking his nose.

High Stool Hornpipe

*Inspired by a tune of the same name written by the artist
and composer, Joe Boske*

High on the pub's high stool the poet sits,
Drowning poems by the pint, supping stanzas,
Iambic pentameters of Guinness, trochees of malt,
Spondees of lager chased down with sips of assonance.

Tomorrow, after the black stool and the fry
He will search his pockets for the sonnets he has swilled.
As much use as look for the leaves that fell last year,
Or go searching for the wind out in the field.

And there on the high stool is the high painter,
Downing noggins of still lives,
Magnums of landscapes, firkins of portraits,
Balloons of abstraction, surreal schooners.

In the morning, with the head Monsignor Bushmills
Has given him, he will scour blank canvases
For visions he has supped.
          As much use look for the steam from off his piss
In last night's Connemara air as, agog, he ogled
The Northern Lights, shimmying like his sister Kate.

On the high stool the piper stares
In real time at his mirrored echo,
Drinking down, jig-time, the crotchets and the quavers;
Drowning crans and rolls, whole reels
And hornpipes, washed down slithering with the slides
And slip jigs down his maw, as the moon glides,
Between the jigs and the reels, over the horns of the bay.

Next day, in the morning's katzenjammer,
When the cats are jamming at the
Dustbin's feline *fleadh ceol*,
He will search his jacket for the music he has lost.
        As much use look for the half-set he has left
Under the old high stool.

There, the cleaner of the morning with her brush
Will find it, coated with the gentle, harmless, dust
Of jumbled, fractured poetry,
The cracked and peeling pigments of lost visions,
The dotted crotchets of un-fingered, stillborn tunes.
And, as she moves the pipes, she hears a noise
And peeps and looks, then bending down,
Ear close, she listens. And the finely dwindling dust
Is lilting in a small and fading voice, reel-time,
'We could have been – we might have been – we should have been...'

The Festival Of Commonsense

You are cordially invited to
The Festival of Commonsense.
There you will meet men in grey faces
Wearing pink newspaper suits who will sell you
Insurance lollies, hedge fund sundaes
And Charlie Ponzi Hokey Pokey –
'One Lick And You'll Stick.' And don't forget
The off-shore, funny money, milk-the-system shakes.

There will be meat and two-faced bread-
And-circus Disneyburgers and
Work until you drop cakes,
At the Festival of Commonsense.

There will be turn-over pension-fund pudding,
Nest-egg omelettes,
And skating on thin ice sorbet,
With Agent Orange sauce
And sprinklings of official statements
At the Festival of Commonsense.

There will be red haired famous people
Famous for being famous,
And an exhibition of people making exhibitions
Of themselves.
Doctors will be spun,
And for the musical, accounts will be fiddled, but quietly
So as not to disturb the Status Quo.

There will be precision bombing pudding
And thermonuclear bon bons,
Napalm nougat and market force mints
And we all sing 'Doh, Ray, Me, Me, Me, Me Me...'
At the Festival of Commonsense;
At the Festival of Commonsense,
Coming constantly to a town near you
To which we are all commanded.

The Way Of Things

And this you think will be the way of things
For ever: the leather satchel ready for the day,
The sandwiches in greaseproof paper, four
Boiled sweets, an apple; snug against
The jotter, the French book, and the pencil-
Case with pens and compass and the chemistry stencil.
The way of it forever, stretching out along
An avenue of warm September days,
To a future that your schoolboy's mind can't hold.

How could you ever see there'd come the day
There'd be no satchel hanging from the hook,
Gaping open for the day ahead?
The sandwiches not made, the house itself
The home of strangers, and all gone, dead,
All scattered to the winds? How could you know
As your inky fingers clutched your bus-
Pass and the money for a playtime drink,
That this instead would be the way of things?

Harry and Fritz

The Crown Inn, Horton in Ribblesdale, 1983

In a desert schooling, forty-odd years past,
They had tried to kill each other in the Libyan sands;
Boy enemies in khaki shorts. Now, pints in hand,
They spy each other through the bottom of a glass.

Had the gunnery been better or the bomber true,
Perhaps one or both would now be sun-picked bones,
The croquet hoops of a rib cage rising through
The Tobruk sand, skull domes mimicking the stones.

Instead, this winter's night, Dales pub, they sup
Their beer; old men, with snaps yellowed with age
Showing grinning boys in forage caps astraddle a camel,
A tank, and they thank God for the gunner's lousy aim,

The truant bomb, and marvel at the madness of it all.
'Too many good lads gone. We were lucky, that's a fact
Fritz'. 'Jah, too many Harry, too many poor lads gone.'
'Fucking politicians Fritz.' 'Jah Harry, I vill drink to that.'

Spillikins

Back of the old settee – deep, elbow in,
While searching for the lost TV remote –
I find a single Jack Straw, spillikin,
And the room is suddenly a swamp of ghosts;
And I am drowning, lost, because
Of a simple, scarlet pick-up stick.

And you can forget your true cross
Splinter in its gold and crystal casket,
This relic sings of other things, things lost,
A greater totem, locally tragic.
A family once sat on that self-same rug
One winter's night before the fire
With a small teepee of spillikins.
Thirty years on the world has turned,
The rug is frayed and faded,
And freckled with small cinder burns.

If ever I come face to face with what great fool
Made all of this, I will furl a knotted noose of Time
And coil it round his throat
And drag him screaming through the burning years
For giving and for taking away
The simple telling of that four
That sat that night, fire-warmed, breath-still,
Edging out the shaking, perilous spills,
The shaking Jack Straw's Castle
Of the times that were to come.

These are the things they couldn't see:
The black, back-alley of the gibbering soul,
The locked ward and the bottled dream machines;
The knives and the green gowns;
The speeding car that spun the small boy through
The air and out of time; the parchment-covered
Death's head barking out its last sharp breaths
Confused and staring in a snare of drips and wires;
The jangle of skin and bones, her memory wiped
Who sits and talks to the TV all day long.

One simple spillikin, and I begin again,
Poor Old Michael Finnigan,
To grieve for all those days that Time,
That thief of the world, has Indian-given
And has snatched back into endless night.

Too Long A Winter

We stumble, stagger on through days that come
Sour and raggy, cruel as armies, sluicing down the dale;
And now, with clay-clag and cold we are numb
And dumb to do anything other than mutter pale

Weak platitudes. Three solid months
Of wet and wind. Clutches of sheep bunch,
Dissolve into the veils of rain; the river takes
Command of roads, and lanes become lakes;

The sky, the dark breast of a settling carrion
Crow, nestles on the land. Not one
Splinter of sun, not one beam or glint, but day
On day of punishing rain and shroud-grey

Skies. We limp on through the days, huddle by fires.
Coughs wrack; children, heads full of snot,
Are nangy and fretful. We search our souls' mire
For sins that might have brought this rot,

This slow, nagging, grey, cold, wet and cruel
Dance of days that we can only stagger through.

Mermaid's Tears

The people of the Island of Iona used to call the perfectly round quartz pebbles they found on the beach 'Mermaid's Tears'

Curmudgeonly Columba, book-thief,
On Iona ambled, eyes inching along
The sea's slippery level, scrying for the smudge
Of Ulster. In the surf, half on, half off a rock
A sea lass, not vain-busy with her hair,
No glass and comb, hands clasped instead in prayer.
She sought, she said, a soul.

       The saint she thought
Could intercede with the maker of all
Mermaids, mermen, monks and seals,
And God would grant her wish.
But fish – decided Columb, heart numb, mind on vellum
Quill and gall (not even all fish but half-woman, half-sole!)
Half a soul wouldn't rate. 'Will a skate'
He asked her 'Come to me next and vex
Me with such a plea? And if God grants your rant
And gives fish souls, will cod in shoals
Howl in Limbo, cry that they died unbaptised?'

       He stared again to sea
Searching for the elusive, emerald smear
Of Ireland on the edge of vision. Then the tears
Began to fall, soundless at first,
But the caoining came and she outsang the
Waves as they lashed the penitential rocks.

And her tears, as they tumbled from her eyes
Ran down her breasts, her belly and her scaly tail,
And turned to faultless, stone spheres; scattering,
Perfect quartz pearls, sweeping out to fill the littorals,
Rattling under the incoming flakes of foam.
They clacked and crackled under cruel Columb's feet
As he staggered back amongst the froth and bladderwrack,
His habit round his segged and saintly knees.
He stumbled on the mermaid's freshly minted tears
Covering his saintly, monkish ears;
Not understanding that a thing that weeps,
As surely as there is a God, must have a soul.

Misericord Carver

In a world lit only by fire, his last
Tense tap teased out a curl of red-gold oak
And hollowed the scoop of the ladle with which the scold
Hammers her husband's head, a fist of beard fast

In her grip; Gyp the dog, arse-up in the pot,
Getting the best of it, while the snug
Domestic scene, world upside-down, erupts
Into all Hell. Next stall, Reynard the Fox

Is lynched by a mob of righteous fowl, chickens and geese,
All beady-eyed and cackling in triumph.
And I rub the wood, feeling the plump
Nub of the murderous woman's cheek,

The bristles of Bold Reynard's brush. Just
So would the carver all those centuries before
Have knowingly stroked his work. Time spans the touch,
And fingers read the carver's braille, more

Subtle than any words. Now feel this pot,
This cheek, this goose, this dangling fox,
And understand how Time with all its multi-coloured dance,
Is nothing but the work of days and hands.

Heritage

A plough, a butter churn, a child's gas mask,
Lace bobbins and a wooden loom;
Flotsam and jetsam of the recent past,
Washed by the tide of Time are fetched up in this room.

A dolly tub, a sandstone quern,
A gelding iron, a first war private's cap,
A hag stone, crystal set, a blunderbuss,
Flint arrow heads, a rag rug, an eel trap,

A linesman's lamp; all the ways we were
Somehow collide in this old school
As though a scattering of refugees
Were gathered random from the years

And then pooled willy nilly, bric-a-bracked here,
Sloughed off like the past's dry skin.
And we stand curious before it all,
As though, by chance, we've stumbled in

To a forgotten attic of the tribe.
For we must accord them reverence somehow,
These brass blow lamps, hay rakes,
Peat spades and weavers' clogs,
Sensing the gravity of these artifacts;
Knowing the hands that touched them
Have left them with a patina of griefs
And innocence and laughter;
The unutterably weighty narrative of the years.

Their relics lie here looking just as though
Those that owned and used them
Have only gone out for a little while,
And will return again to weave and spin,
And plough and wash and scrub, and sit
In the hedge carpenter's chair before the fire
And tune the old valve radio in before turning,
To smile at us across the room of years.

The Fifth Dimension

We plot and chart our course co-ordinates
And comb the coastline with the radar's emerald sweep;
While, on the sea's lip, Lucifer glimmers,
And the plough, on its axle of ice,
Turns slow above the mast.
Astrolabe, sextant, compass,
Depth-sound, plumb-line, asdic,
Sonar, satnav, azimuth; with them all
We box the compass, mark our point,
Take soundings, find true north, dead reckoning –
Our position thus, star-struck, fixed,
Hammered to the nanosecond
Rock firm, solid, in the matrix.

But how will you, mariner, measure
The other sea in which we all swim blind and lost:
The fifth dimension, Love,
Through which we trawl our comical days?
Without it what do all our riches buy –
As we coast the oceans riding on a Midas wave?

Empty castles, echoing mansions,
Halls echoing and cold,
Where the rats of doubt skitter before you
Scattering the mould.
What will you have?
Dross, dust, coffers of scented nothing,
Grand estates of bugger-all.

Without that other simple, plain co-ordinate,
In spite of all our reckonings,
Our bloated argosies return
Their holds chock full of fools' gold,
Making barren landfall
On a hopeless archipelago.

The Bookseller of Baghdad

*In memoriam Mohammed Hayawi, bookseller, 'a bald
bear of a man'*

He sat, sipping his sweet, black, tea, as the wreath of smoke
From his Gauloise coiled, spooled, broke
And faded. He was framed by shelf on shelf
Of books, a catacomb of fading spines, time itself
Fading; the tick, tick, tock of words
Waiting to be read. He said, 'All that matters is that books
Be there, a great unending sea of thoughts,
Truth somewhere to be found. Most all we know
Is written down; talk flies, the printed page
Remains. It is the best that we can do.
Mapmakers, poets and the history men;
The storytellers and the wise they lead
Us into other worlds and other ways.
And yet it lacks perfection's surety;
Perhaps that is the way that it should be.
For tell me now,' this wise man smiled,
'Is there anybody who, with not one flea
Of doubt to itch his mind,
Can tell me exactly all that happened yesterday?
Or what will come tomorrow?
And even be so sure of what is now?'
He threw the question to the warm air with his hand,
Smoke gloved it. Outside a lemon seller sang
His ware's freshness as he pushed his cart.
'Listen to that lemon seller. In a few years he'll be gone,
His cart and lemons and his stories too.
We pass like smoke, like shadows from dark to dark.'

Then, as somewhere off, a stray dog barked,
The street of the shops of books assumed a different life.
As the bomb burst, paper, bindings, boards, glass, lights,
Livers and lungs, words, soft flesh, chapters,
Skin, endpapers, entrails, fingers, bindings, bone
And thread became a great mosaic of meat and texts. And still
And slow the Tigris went its way, meandering now,
Its narrative marbled with fresh blood and ink.
Pages and body parts, floated, bobbed, only to sink.
Sirens howled, dust swirled, men ran.
And stories in ink and paper, stories in bone and blood,
Were making their way to the sea, following the flood.
And the books and the bookseller were now just
Words and flesh, and spooling, heavenward smoke
That curled and turned, frayed, faded and finally broke.

The Blackbird

I knew no better then, my ten-year ears
Had only heard these songs: sparrows, pigeons,
Cats, budgies, dogs and old Reg full of beer
Rattling the lugs of the midnight, dustbinned streets.

Here, walking back through after-school
Suburban roads, a somewhere blackbird sang
The summer's evening down. And I had never heard
Music so wonderful, a song that soaked into my bones.

Round those still, sycamore streets it spooled;
I stood and listened to it stitch its song into the dying day;
Liquid, fluting round those quiet, warm avenues
Reaching out and threading Time itself,

As though there never was, nor ever had
Been anything other than this song.
And then I knew what beauty truly was,
And knew why old men cried.

Signalman Crossing Blea Moor

Night thickens, gathers, weaves together sky and fell
As you leave the road and strike across the moss.
Stars splinter into life, and the first frost-
Blisters skin the puddles, glisten on the gutter edge.

From the mouth of the tunnel,
Sudden, a shunting Black Five thunders
Backwards, comes in a clatter, spewing sparks
That school and swirl, echoing the stars.

Two men, unmoving statues, brass-bright,
Are frozen in the footplate firelight.
They carry the sun on south
Into the night, a hooting iron owl,

Its feathers a link of gibbering wagons.
The lit box calls, you dander on,
Ice on your moustache, every sleeper a year,
Sixty three of them. You step with care

Timing your pace to their space, still bound,
As you have been since school, to the steel path
And the unbending iron. A frost ring around
The rising moon, ice spangles in your breath.

A fav off lorry trundles down the dale,
As that griping pain clenches yet again in your chest,
You stop to catch your breath on the signal box steps,
And the starlight falls like rain upon the rails.

Shoot-out At The OK Bombsite

Celluloid dreams drove us across
The Monument Valley of our streets,
Whooping Roy Rogers in short socks,
Dodging the cougars of the alley cats.

Wheels spinning backwards,
The covered wagon (the rag and bone man's
Horse and cart) headed across the cobbled salt lake.
In our backyard coal sheds we cowhands
Fashioned forty-fives from clothes pegs,
Lee Enfields carved from firewood
With the smuggled-out breadknife.

Heading down the summer-warm streets,
We slapped our holiday arses and galloped
To the bombsites; an Apache in every wash-house
And Comanches by the chip shop lay in wait.
The Sioux were riding down the cobbled lanes,
And the Navaho lay in ambush by the Methodist chapel gates.

Yet, in that made-up world real terror lurked,
For, stray too far into the other tribal lands,
And trouble lay in wait: kicks and half bricks,
Punches, thumps, Chinese burns and worse.

It was a whisper of the grown-up years to come,
With its new badlands of dark alleys and bombsites,
Where even Hopalong would be afraid,
Trapped between the Dead Man's Gulch and home.

The Firewood Bird

One day I made a bird of firewood,
Copper wire and paper wings, it looked good
To me standing in our backyard;
A heron, aloof, intent,
Scrying imaginary, mossy frogs
In the shallow waters of the Yorkstone flags.

Next afternoon, school done I brought my friend to see
My wonderful bird, but it was gone,
Set free by my father's fire, who could not see
A bird in sticks and paper. My firewood bird
Set free, fluttered high above our street,
Dark wings of smoke, feathers of ash
Soaring above the rooftops in the November rain.

A Month of Angry Skies

A month of angry skies and still,
New lambs lig on hail, they yarl for dams
That sniff the wind, sensing ice. Clouds
Spill and rear up pawing at the light; the sun
Hangs low, a pewter blister on the world's black rim.
Storm coming, the sheep paw the earth, nervous, tired,
Long winter curdling into sour spring.
Dead lambs and yowes melt into the sodden earth,
By walls, rot where they fall.

Against the black clouds picked out by the sexton sun
On the dark hill, sheep are foam flecks on the moss,
Maggots on Helm Knott's giant corpse. Only
The crows are gorged and rattle cackling,
Sated black chevrons roosting in the winter sticks.
Beyond, the Howgills lurk,
Their colours muted, drained, pale,
Merging thumb-rubbed into the carrion sky.
Yowes yarl, and new lambs lig on hail.

The River Rehearses Its Grammar

The river rehearses its grammar, chanting
Down the dale; rote-fashion; singing school
By trout pools, under elders and sagged willows,
While we, word blind, code-less,
Watch it construe its way towards the sea.
Its long tongue stumbles on shoals,
Trips on weed-haired boulders under alders,
Prattles over pebble beds where dippers delve,
Pools where trout the colour of a sunset lurk
And hunting deep in the bowels of the foss,
Booms out its thunderous ultimatum;
Rehearsing in these nithered, cramped moorland crags,
Cantos of uncaged skies, rock pools and gulls to come.

Setting Free The Birds

Glacial scars on granite cut no deeper than
The memories of you in white lace tights,
Tottering, your hair in bunches, pushing a toy pram.
Ink on vellum; no more lasting than your sister
Stopping half turned in the kitchen door to sniff
The open coffee jar, her eyes closed in a smile,
Filled suddenly with some inner, wordless, joy.
This time capsule within the skull
Holds more than any museum.

You know, the hardest thing is letting go;
Not power, position, money, show,
But children, small ones you have held
And cradled, nursed and led
By hand to parks and swings and taught
To walk along the singing stave,
To clap, to talk, to dance.

Letting go of the child who turned
Burning in the door, smiling, aflame
In the sun, happy at something:
A sound, a bell, a book, a candle?

They can not see how much you burn
For them, and that is how it is;
The young are filled with light,
Why should we lay the shadows on them?

Yet it comes hard, the breaking.
But so it goes, and so they go,
Slipping from the harbour of your heart,
Your little vessels. You must cast them off

Knowing that, in the uncaring waves
Of bitter seas, they will be alone.
And, with the storms beyond the bar,
You shred the very fabric of your soul,
Stand on the darkened, wintry, quay,
And let the rope of tears slide out to sea.

In Praise of Frost

Moss, glutted on a month of rains,
Baulks at the now grey, sodden air that seems
So clagged with mist that we
Breathe water, swim down all the days,

Sit by the fireside, staring out at a drowned world;
Liquid, brozen with wet. The great sponge of the fells
Fills syke and beck and we hang on,
And hope for sun, mites on the dale's dropsical skin.

November, and for weeks the earth and sky
Have been subsumed and turned fluid; the crags
Have grown slick skins of slime threatening
A melt down. Nothing is real in this pre-natal world,

And secretly we, amniotic, pray for days of frost
For frozen, brittle sticks rattling above solid pools,
Ice-crusted ruts, breath smoking in the morning air
And the sun a pale, dry blister on the lip of the eastern fell.

Two Irish Tunes

1 – MY DARLING ASLEEP

For P

In this small continent of a room
All history distils itself into the folds
Of stockings cast upon the chair,
The bra and knickers tumbled to the floor.
All philosophy is in your shape
Curled, comma-like under the sheets
Sleeping out this summer night.
And I stand at the window
Listening to the breathing town;
The world shrunk to a dog's bark;
The wind tangling with the trees;
The full moon hustling through
The rag-and-bone shop of the clouds.
And I know that God itself,
That all of Time, all understanding,
Is in your every breath.

2 – THE LARK ON THE STRAND

'Singing its heart out,' once they would have said,
But poets now know better, and they bin
Words like 'heart' and 'love' searching
For the truth in irony and tone instead.

Yet here upon the strand – Atlantic combers shrunk
To a lapping on the shore – a speck, a dribble
Of feathers, blood and bone, sings out its heart, drunk
With joy, writing, across this Donegal bay, scribbles

Of delight. My soul in shreds, I walk
The healing shore beneath a sky
Where poetry falls like summer snow,
From the throat of a skywinding lark.

Somebody Shot The Angels

Somebody shot all the angels,
Knocked them right out of the sky,
Took them off the rooftops with a catapult,
Vaporised them on the sly

With an agnostic ray gun got for Christmas.
Scattered angel pellets round the roses,
Set angel traps, called out
The council angel exterminator. So they're

Gone. Gone the same road as
The Sandman, the Bogeyman,
Jenny Greenteeth, the Tooth Fairy
And Icky the Bare Bum Fire Bobby.

Now from the four corners of the atheistical heavens
No trumpets sound, no feathers flutter, no soft breath
Puffs out the clouds, no plump cherubim,
No hosannas, no glorias, no seraphim,

Just the trail of a jet, smoke from a stack,
And the everyday streets ring to
The canticle of rubber on tarmac, lauds
Of work-bound feet – hosannas of the fallen.

Leaving The Old House

I thought this place an abode of ghosts
Time-trammelled hungers and loves lost,
All calling from the walls and crannies; faces
Staring from the plaster, dusty voices

Whispering; motes of laughter of
Small children coming from above
Somewhere; old Christmas cards,
A cup ring-stain. And yet, as I move through

The house, fill boxes with old books,
Take down the pictures leaving their echoes
Shadowed on the wall, pack half-made poems
Take old coats down from off their hooks,

I see I am the poltergeist, that carries history
From room to innocent room,
Haunting the house; the long days that are gone –
A tribe of monkeys gibbering on my back.

We Learn We Do Not

Emerging blinking into the light, the all-
Clear sounding over the city, war
And the pity of war threw us off kilter –
For a while. Hitler gone, we'd ration cards still to

Buy stuff with, and Uncle Joe building
An iron curtain followed quickly by the Berlin
Wall. And yet we hoped, when the Mau Mau
Boiled up on our screens, that now, at last, somehow

We all had learned and that things
Would get better, in a way, perhaps, you know...
And then the Beatles and the '60s ringing
In a change; Macmillan lampooned, Profumo

Trapped in *Private Eye*'s young net,
The old guard getting toe pie up the arse. And yet
We were drinking in the Old Last Chance Saloon. Was it
A bad moon rising? No just us, letting the lunatics,

Who'd never really gone, take over yet again:
The bankers and the generals that think
They'll give us bread and circuses, and spin
The truth until which way is up is down – again.

They took us for the clowns we are,
And all the deaths were all in vain, still are.
They lie and murder with a fine disdain,
Piss up our backs, and tell us that it's rain.

The New Jerusalem

For the begrudged and minimum hourly
Wage she changes the sheets and the towels
Refills the soaps and shampoos, scours
The toilet pan until its bowl's

Ice white again. Each morning
While this great hotel is heavy with
The smell of breakfast, and yawning
Suited men sit down to dine,

She tidies cleans and dusts and mops
And works around the modems and laptops
Hand made, soft morocco leather cases;
And in the bathroom, aftershaves

And scents and cream for working hands.
And an image comes to her of rough
Sandpaper hands that used to move with desert
Heat across her skin, to wake the heat inside her;

Hard hands weathered by the pick shaft,
Tanned by hods and perfumed by
The tarmac boiler's smoke, hands that
Hang daily now, workless and softening by the fire.

There Were No Colours

'There are no colours.' That is all he said
When the men in jackboots led him from the cell.
'Now I know what hell is like, it is a well
Filled with a lead-grey silence, a widdershin world
Where daylight has been banned, the birds are gagged,
The rainbow is abolished, and time is made to run
All arse-about. The clouds and sky are hidden;
The passing noises of the street locked up,
And the wind's breath in the branches is erased.

So to help you feel at home in your new world
They kindly bring you – dinner at dawn,
Porridge at supper and, in case you fear the dark,
The sun and moon of the lightbulb stays full-risen
Always in your world. The spiders on
The ceiling are the night and day sky stars;
The peeling bricks of your cell wall
The rolling hills of a far-off land.

And now I see, I truly understand
How the generals with their guns and tanks,
The big men with their factories and their banks,
Who tortured me because I didn't see
The world their way, were only trying to show
Me that their eyes see things in shades of black and white.
And now it is as clear as day and night:
That a man who dares to ask for a slice of bread
In a field of corn he used to own is a dangerous thing;
Feral like the truth, a danger to
The state; an antichrist, a communist.

Therefore to make him well and whole again
The universe must be scoured and bleached,
All colours must be cancelled, must be leeched
To the paintbox of despair, the palette of the shroud.
All rainbows, prisms, colours of laughter, joy,
Song, love, care, tenderness and hope
Abolished, by royal and military decree;
Colours declared by government edict,
Signed and countersigned, no longer to exist.

A tortured Chilean intellectual on being released from his cell after months of torture by the Pinochet regime said that he could no longer see colours. He was kept in a silent room with no daylight, a lightbulb burning constantly so that he would not know day from night. To further disorientate him meals were brought at random times, sometimes no more than an hour apart. It took months before his sense of colour came back.

Understanding Heathcliff

Stood looking out on the canal and wharf,
The railway arches and the chimneys
On a cold, drab, soot-brick morning,
I remember the ghost of a terrible grief:
A seven-year-old out alone on a bomb site,
Crying in the lost morning
For a world that had gone and would be no more;
And I want more than anything to open
Wide that bright and clamorous window
To a morning drunk with sunlight
And call that lost child in.

Making The Past

And this is how we make the past: I take
My pen, open the book and write the story of this night.
I write, *This summer's evening slides away*
As the sun slips towards Inishbofin. An Irish Lights

Ship rides at anchor in the half-moon bay
Its dinghy puttering ashore, day
Dies and men head for the Pier Bar,
Joyce's, Oliver's or Newman's for a jar.

And this is how we make the past, we have
No choice; I and Bofin and the brass-bright waves
And the thirsty, shore-bound sailors in the lee,
A corixa, salamander scuttling across a burning sea.

Moone The Poet

It said on the poster in the hotel door,
And inside the precious poet (state of the hearts,
Arts week primed) versified and rhymed before
The stanza-starved and haiku-hungry crowd.

Outside the West of Ireland got on with
Its non-poetry, non-festival, non-arts week way:
Women with late shopping, a farmer with a sick
Calf in a trailer and four muttering men
Manouevering a particularly heavy piece
Of old oak furniture across the busy street.

Perhaps seeing it as a command four little boys
Stood on a bench, and dropped their pants
Then pressed their little bare pink bottoms on the lower panes
Of lounge-room glass, and mooned the poet, Moone,
Who, back to the window and wallowing
Deep in the bogs and abyss of his angst,
Wondered why he was telling the sad tale
Of his seventh nervous breakdown
To a rocking, sweating, snorting, mirth-mad room.

Nighthawks

A street-lark singing in the winter town,
Night crowds parting all around
Her, she stands, a rock in centre stream,
Her song half chant, half caoin.

Seven plastic bags about her carry her
Whole world, a supermarket bag
For every decade of her life; her history –
Seven sorrowful mysteries: the Stage,
Stardom, the booze, the lovers crossed;
The slide, the ruined voice, the money lost.
She sings her song into the night, notes
Slicing through the motes
Of starlings in the neon city sky,
Drowning the far off traffic. *Bye*
Bye Blackbird; slow, she dribbles
Lusciously over every syllable, sucking
Them like pebbles before blowing them out
In bubbles of sweet sound.

Upon the warming cellar grating, lit
By a window of suited dummies, her audience sits,
His world in a paper bag, from which he drinks
The oceans, drowns the stars. His eyes are back
In Alamein, his dreams in Alexandria.
He mutters curses and he sees
A Glasgow churchyard in his mind's eyes
And a name that hasn't touched his lips for years.

Then, sweeter than woodsmoke on a winter's night,
Softer than the breeze amongst the chapel trees,
Gentler than any petal falling on the grass,
She sings half-tempo to an emptying street,
A song of loneliness, of parting and of home.

The night winds hurry the dust
And old chip-papers round the square,
A cat trots on its shadow, off somewhere;
And to the moon, to the empty playground swings,
And to the man who lives in bottles,
With her trash-can clothes and matted hair
The madonna of the middens sings,
And the night is suddenly ablaze with beauty.

Siege

Eighty-four years old, and yet he's at it still
In the field above my house in the raw spring dawn;
Raking down mole castles that were built
In the first night of this late spring-coming thaw –

Fresh earth piles, pustules to his mind.
And in the old accustomed round he finds
Their tunnels, sleeving them with his sprung steel
Traps. There's no stock now on his tumbled fields,

The bank owns every blade of grass. And yet the dance
Leads him out into this glassy morning for the kill;
The mist strewn ragged in the branches
Of the river trees, washing half-way up the hill,

Leaving us islanded. And out he goes yet to the slaughter.
'London brass' will have his land. Owd Mowdiwarp.
He lays siege to his neighbours in their clay clochans,
Easing his back and straightening up to hear the clatter

Of the hedge fund's helicopter hovering overhead,
A slim, steel tube surveying his lonely acres,
Mapping, measuring – and missing everything;
Not seeing how, hand on hand, these walls, this land
Was made; failing to read the rubric of the dale that makes
Each stone an epic, each won field a litany of the dead.

Van De Welde In The Empty Quarter

Dutch painters took the sky and made it customary;
Expansive, not without its charm; sometimes
Looming, curdled with cloud; impressive,
Iconic, not without its grandeur, yet also
Somehow familiar, commonplace.
They framed in even its braggadocio
At sea, when luggers slewed off the canvas' edge,
And slabs of waves – instant Alps – rose up,
To sag and slip and slide away again.
                    Inland, high trees
Lead the eye to a vastness blue and finite
That caps the flatlands; and comely, mercantile
Holland with its fat barques, its certainties,
Its booze, its pancakes, dogs and wedding bagpipes,
Celebrating churns and tiles and sinks – abolishes eternity.

But nothing could prepare you for this sky,
This battering blue, this cobalt savagery
That cauls the desert; an emptiness that exists
Only to suck the juices from you
Like a hagfish, and then blow
You husked and sloughed, all bones and dust,
Into the edge of frame. Nothing makes
You more an alien than these skies:
Not the scorpions, not the sand,
Not the oasis, widdershins in the air,
Flexing, Hi Brazil above the land;
But the sky, where water has never
So much as been a whisper.
                    A saint perches
Crow-like on a pillar, praying that the sun
Will suck him up to heaven. And all around
The sands stretch, melting under this
Levelling sky, where kings and merchants,
Burghers and beggars, queens, sea captains,

Wedding guests and seascape painters – all
Are tiny shucks, motes, specks, humbled,
Tumbled by the scorched, indifferent winds;
A universe away from luggers and white horses,
Loaded argosies riding in the offing,
Wet canvas luffed against a dropsical northern sky.

Old School Photograph

In memoriam Fr Augustus (Foxy) Reynolds: St Bede's
College: Manchester

It rolled out of a box of ends and odds:
A dead-see scroll. Forty-odd years on.
I flattened it out, a book on either end,
And peeled the years back like a bandage from a wound.

Now a matrix of young faces looks from out
The rummage box of Time. But who is who?
The bully, informer, best friend, torturer, swot;
The saint, the whited sepulchre, the fool,

The pedant, pederast, grey man, the misanthrope,
The mystic, innocent – even the murderer perhaps?
I search the faces, fetched up on the shoals of years
For traces, post holes, crop marks, but give up hope.

Half a dozen in the rows of heads I name,
And memory simmers: wet towels slapping backs,
Punches given, great goals scored, April Fool
Tricks bringing Lenten purple to the faces of the great.

And they, the front row, the Monsignor and
The masters; only they, soutaned rocks against the years'
Undoing are unchanged: Willy, Prune, Wild Bill, Foxy,
Hambone, Fudge, Tojo, Bandy
And Spike; their sins and graces known
Only to a thinning band of balding Magi.

The boys are gone. Whatever chrysalids,
Imagoes once were there, the years have hatched,
And I see only history's husks as I trawl for names;
A mariner scanning a strange constellation
In a new hemisphere. Forty years and more
The tides have scoured and shifted. Now
Six hundred strangers stare at me out of
A summer's black and white, lost, panorama day.

The Colossi Do A Runner

From The Gastro-pub At The End Of The Cosmos

*'In the old days they called it embezzlement; now they
call it bonuses.'*

ANON

They bestrode the Universe, Creation Lords,
Bred to the bone, the natural inheritors;
We meekly bowed our heads to receive their swords
Content to let the Great Ironicals rule over us.

We learn from History both words and tune,
And yet we never join them up to make the song,
Believing perhaps that now, this time, our ruin
Will not be so severe or last so long.

Fools led by donkeys, clayfoot idiots painted gold
By the braying paper men. We got on the bus,
'More! More! Have more – you're worth it!' Sold
The pup, we wondered why it grew to savage us.

And when we, Oz-like, looked behind the screen
We saw the Giants, Colossi, for the dwarves they were,
By then it was too late and the suited men, the breed
Of cheap buffoons had scarpered, were no longer there.

You historians of the future mark this down,
That when the bread and circuses hit town,
There were others of us who refused to go
And join the madness of that magical, mystery show,

That saw the Emperor's arse and his feet of clay,
The wizard's gaudy speaking tube, his magic pill;
That saw the simpering waiters totting up the bill,
And knew the pigs who troughed the most would not be there to pay.

Abandoned Allotment Sheds

Lancashire 1973

Corrugated iron roofs, warped, twisted beams
Housed some men's fantasies and hopes,
While others fettled up small workaday dreams
From old doors, skirting boards and creosote;

Settled on a stock-brick base, tarpaper felt,
And spider-frosted, second-hand glass.
Yet all the sheds, shimshank or crafted, still were built
It seems with something of a view to last.

The mill that wove the weft and warp
Of all their days is standing yet above it all:
The canal, the allotments, the silted wharf;
Yet it too, now, is waiting for the wrecker's ball.

Raddled by rain, islanded by nettles,
The sad sheds lurch and lean over the abandoned plots,
Lichened wooden trays, seized sprays, holed kettles,
Rain-butts, rotted riddles and cracked pots.

All around, the returning army of the thistles claims
The land again, seed heads shiver in the wind then flit,
Go scattering from their bloody helmets
Sewing the battalions to come down all the days.

And standing yet, the abandoned sheds, their doors
Awry, paint gone, they hang on half a hinge;
Roofs holed, the sunlight falls through dust to rotting floors.
This day the summer sky is a soft, blue scrim,

The air is thick and warm and clotted with the boom
Of bees that clamber in the mouths of blooms
Now run to weed; and all the work of days and hands is done.
Men's little sheds, patched with such care and love.

Summer's evenings, after work, the smoke
From fags and pipes fending off haloes
Of midges, they would talk of mould and rot
And bluestone sprays around the water butts.
On winter dawns they footed up potato drills,
Their breath a fine gold smoke, the sun
A new bright copper coin rising through mist
On the canal.
            But, these days, no men come,
And day on day the sheds slide slowly back
To earth, weeds smudge the lines between the plots,
And once-prized plants throw up green arms,
All bolted, gone to seed, lost in the dock,
The dandelions and the jungle grass. Days pass,
And the men now are an emptiness,
A breath not taken, a husk of silence, a song
No longer sung. The allotments go to pot,
Run riot, waiting for the dozers rant,
The footings, shuttering, the concrete shroud,
The breezeblock castles of the new executive estate.

Soon children of the years to come will stand
At windows watching rain blow down grey avenues,
Never to know that here, once, men smoked pipes
While pricking seedlings tenderly out with leather thumbs,
Snipping cuttings with a father's ground-down blade,
In hot, small, quiet, ramshackle sheds that smelled
Of creosote, tobacco smoke and allotment dreams,
That they had made; green dreams in a green shade.

Slipway

There is nothing beyond this last grey spur of land
But the darkness of the gathering night.
Nothing moving but the world's great old skin
Slackly rising and falling, whispering amongst
The tangled trails of bladderwrack,
Burnishing the barnacled rocks; they shine in the dock lights.

There is nobody, a cat leaping a barrel is all.
Nothing, except that, far out beyond the bay,
There will be sailors leaning on the rail,
On watch, staring at our harbour lights, perhaps,
And looking down at the sussuration of foam
Capping the wash, their sea-heavy heads
Bucketful of dreams of fair women and soft beds.

There is nowhere beyond until the pack ice,
Jigsaw of the coast, and the fretwork fjords of
Greenland locked in winter half the year.

There is nothing more but the journey,
There is nowhere else but the path,
And tonight no boat will come
Clamorous with light and laughter to this harbour.

Luath Press Limited
committed to publishing well written books worth reading

LUATH PRESS takes its name from Robert Burns, whose little collie Luath (*Gael.*, swift or nimble) tripped up Jean Armour at a wedding and gave him the chance to speak to the woman who was to be his wife and the abiding love of his life. Burns called one of 'The Twa Dogs' Luath after Cuchullin's hunting dog in Ossian's *Fingal*. Luath Press was established in 1981 in the heart of Burns country, and is now based a few steps up the road from Burns' first lodgings on Edinburgh's Royal Mile.

Luath offers you distinctive writing with a hint of unexpected pleasures.

Most bookshops in the UK, the US, Canada, Australia, New Zealand and parts of Europe either carry our books in stock or can order them for you. To order direct from us, please send a £sterling cheque, postal order, international money order or your credit card details (number, address of cardholder and expiry date) to us at the address below. Please add post and packing as follows: UK – £1.00 per delivery address; overseas surface mail – £2.50 per delivery address; overseas airmail – £3.50 for the first book to each delivery address, plus £1.00 for each additional book by airmail to the same address. If your order is a gift, we will happily enclose your card or message at no extra charge.

Luath Press Limited
543/2 Castlehill
The Royal Mile
Edinburgh EH1 2ND
Scotland
Telephone: 0131 225 4326 (24 hours)
Fax: 0131 225 4324
email: sales@luath.co.uk
Website: www.luath.co.uk